One Last Ditch

Erik J. M. Schneider

a t e l o s
3 2

One Last Ditch

with amazement
for
Nan and Karl

Contents

minutes overtime

when Chicago was far enough
not to imagine or only to. which
reminds me
it is not that association gets you nowhere.
or it is
but gaping impractically. or more than the sage
punctual
like the pulse of a glock
all the way to that shelf where instant gathers into shade.
the best of distance brought
not home exactly.
base 10 written
the shine on an electron
the talk strained at its circular run
manufactured extruded steel. they will dig here
cynical pickaxes pulverizing veins liver and heart.

between torn tissue the veil rent also
holiest holes dank and bitter
give up the ghost steamed in modest portions.
varnish the truth seal it up
good. a paneled cell holding the perfect thief.
thrown in for good measure:
a pewter stein with a hunting motif—
receptacle for relief.
you always forget to
make it brief. rare earth
science names you
names keep you
the keep will hold you
until escape
excuses itself remanding the breach here.
a bus shudders where no one could see
the course is frayed so remain composed
faithfully estranged.
were it to stop. but no—
you'll arrive fashionably late
dressed to the nines.

exurb

there is no good reason why when upon seeing houses in
neat rows with lawns and sidewalks and trees and cars in
the driveways and basketball nets on the walls and fuchsias
at the corners of the gardens and nothing much all around
except quiet isolation from the neighbors there is no good
reason why when I see all this I only feel dread as though
suspended over each lawn were a wheel for breaking
bodies and which were fired up each day at 3:30 in the
afternoon and ran until midnight or at least just after
dinner when the calm of the stomach took over and drew
us slipping into night and dreams and the sanctuary three
by six which would hold you until light broke and we
would tumble out of the houses and past the wheels that
were not there and on.

ode, continued

to slake.
to sulk.
to lack.
to reckon.

to caress.
to rescue.
to curse.
to scream.

to sup.
to press.
to spray.
to rasp.
to spur.

i could go on.

to cull.
to lapse.
to spell.
to list.
to sterilize.

to trace.
to tow.
to wager.
to keep watch.
to speak legions.
to wreak heaven.

to wrack
to rack
to reek
to wreck.

to cast off.

to forage.
to grouse.
to rage.
to grovel.
to veil.

verisimilitude. where does it all come from.

to dredge.
to redress.
to sort.
to twist.
to thrash.
to retch.
to chart.
to crate.

to excel.
to collate.
to alter.

to instigate latency.
to gloss.
to slug.
to greet the slovenly.

to hesitate.

siege at times

intermittent backlash. one hour two hours three hours
four but no more. it becomes clear after awhile here the
rafters smile but it becomes clear that they've reared
just what they meant to and then again not. enormous
misfire in fact if wracked in the way i thought when i
was young i was going to hell no matter what i did no
matter what was said to me no matter if i did precisely
what was read to me and it's no wonder.

well it's no wonder and i wonder. if all the names of
history are to deposit their trash on my doorstep what
am i supposed to do with it. there is no sanity except in
the choosing of delusions so choose yours and so choose.
i could use another moment of sheer youth as they say or
as he says as who says it doesn't matter i say sheer youth.
in the morning with first coffee forgetting who we are

until it all filters back and there you are under it. it's no wonder.

let me at it.

benzodiazepine

where the confusion lies. where does the confusion lie. most probably the most confusion lies in the most compulsive of ideas. most probably the most confusion is in the idea itself.

dispersal and infinition. waiting long enough will bring it all. which is to say there is no wait long enough and there is no all but waiting and dispersal. patience and release. the compulsive in reverse.

cryptorchid

i have gone round and round with this trying both to catch it and stay out of its way.

there was a time when there was no guard he said. you could walk right through to the other side and no one would stop you or ask you to explain what you were doing there.

only a heretic could bear it and i did. being brought up short is its own reward but so is being whipped. a certain precision follows but at whose expense.

dehydration. functioning nonetheless carried on. a hundred demons and a hundred exorcists and what the hell. towheaded when small signals of susceptibility at some later date. as though nothing were. we went appalled grinning at the lapses possible. synapses tolerable but one could say that and no more. brought up daily.

so thoroughly sorted one by one and one by one. pick it up and put it down only slightly displaced. here we go. again and again.

white noise

litter.
calamitous.
falsifiable.
alternator.
mend.
portly.
flee.
westerly.
magnetism.
stricken.
carp.
vaunted.
maritime.
aloft.
defer.
nip.

name that tune

a c.s. lewis book. not the screwtape letters but something else.

the banality of evil. lucifer and jehovah are the same. heresy. evil is the province only of animal instinct run amok.

worn but expensive shoes. what is it like to have to shave at 18.

this man won't get out of the doorway even though there is empty space all around him.

if i sit on a particular side i run less risk of head injury in the event of a major earthquake. likewise if i sing ashes to ashes while underwater we will make it to the other side unscathed.

sometimes i sing something different just to try the fates.

how much can you pile on one handtruck. a livelihood apparently.

a quick repair in the space of a quarter-mile. he made it. every destination is important.

don't just stand at the top of the escalator. at the other end she yelled at no one and everyone looked uncomfortable but she did not notice at all.

one thing i have learned is that racing bikes and mountain bikes have different gear ratios. i am not sure why i study them but i do.

do my hips look like hers or his or something in between. that man's pants are very flat.

marvelous how well-aligned the new stickers are. most of them. i've been in this car twice this week i can tell because i recognize the wrinkle.

always the same guy asking for eighty-five cents. how does he get in without a ticket. charity interrupted by timidity. i knew someone once who was unbelievably rude.

what will be the fate of that section of the paper. will it know the difference. i have been coming here for six years and still i feel the dislocation.

now i can go anywhere. this was all it took.

i finally figured out the smell was from a bread factory which is funny because she had told me long ago that it smelled like bread.

not at rush hour. for many reasons not the least of which is a chair.

the same shirt three days in a row. whether he realizes it or not we compete for the place at the front. i don't know why i do it.

there is a way to avoid fumbling i would like to tell them all but not everyone can be efficient. walk when going down but stand still when going up. it is the only logical method.

dimes often don't work at first but if you follow them with a nickel they'll pass on through. why is it so difficult. it helps if you crease it just so.

sneak a peek at their shoes. and other parts.

vacancy

caught.
registry.
gimlet.
enamel.
lariat.
radial.
derringer.
interment.
staple.
fructify.
encaustic.
scapula.
lupine.
annunciate.
toss.
sterile.
relict.

a measure whereupon between hiss and steel.

sun.
groan.
rock.
body.
aboard.
rustic.
shoal.
horde.
dredge.
ragged.

click.

crush #15

it was sweat. I recognized it because I had sweated before. there were arms and legs asking to be let through to be moved past and not knowing the etiquette I let them. the question of who is indulgent of whom is not clear when it is also not clear just where on the spectrum between rival and trick the requesting party might stand. I noticed that if I stared too long at for instance that one muscular waist they would stare back and I not being ready to commit looked away.

the arms and legs slipped past and kept slipping past as there was no end to the wanting to go here or there or back again and when the show was over they all rushed for the door hoping I suppose to let the sweat dry a little. then it was a matter of not getting carried away.

but before that before the release of have a good night set

loose their joyful quest for air one by one a kind hand or a discreet knee would make its acquaintance and then press on leaving that mark to smolder in its wake a note of a wish so casual it vanished into the crowd with the moment which called it out.

once standing in a line I let her put her hand on my chest. I didn't know who she was and she was dirty and she was drunk but she was only looking to make friends and asked liquid manners stirring crinkled rimshot eyes palm up can I touch you. ok. lightly her hand on the thin cold layer of my summertime shirt one beat two from far away a rumbling stampede I stepped back her fingers floated alone for a moment she swaying just beneath her own notice. I will never forget her and she will never remember me. either way nothing can come between us or nothing can interpose itself at that one point when nothing came between us.

in the zoo they all sleep in a heap.

it is true that I am a rank novice.

cache

there are still twenty-one penny rolls piled neatly in that triangular order of a certain number under a certain number minus one under a certain number minus two and so on. I keep counting them not because I don't know how many there are but because they invite counting from one flickering spot to the next each flicker not exactly like the last but enough like the last that it counts in the series as one in a series of something countable. counting over and again as though to say to oneself again and over they are there just right there just within grasp and moments later counting begins anew as though they were twenty-two.

were they a field of one thousand. miraculous instance.
you are number six

I noticed the heft and suddenly felt the urge to reinvent the

wheel. metal and its attraction to mostly metal. what
could it mean.

what could it mean.
what precisely exactly and only what.
I smeared myself with mud once it was urgent.
to pass along from the point at which the particular
multiplies under pain of particularity drinking its own
anonymity like morphine.
this one and this one and this one and this one.
not alike in animality but punctual and raw.

courtesy is not enough.

whiz #7

the men's room is deteriorating. not everywhere or at least as far as I know only in this particular spot although probably one could find deteriorating men's rooms elsewhere but here there was a seat and then there was no seat but there was still a stall door but now there is no stall door either and all of this would not be so bad except that the door to the outside opens directly onto a view of the stall and there is no lock on the door to the outside so one crouches trying to hover above the seatless fixture while concentrating on what to do if the door opens for instance does my shirt cover me or do my pants not pulled all the way down cover me or should I move my arms across to cover me because this is always the question how best to cover in order not to evoke great surprise or consternation or urge to kill. and that vulnerable moment between sitting (crouching) and standing where one's only recourse is to turn quickly around and let their eyes reassure them in the absence of continuous corroborating evidence that they did not see what they did not expect to see. that or meeting their eyes with a yes you saw it but that's life you sometimes see odd things and for pete's sake why not let it be.

what's more

we drank on the golf course in the dark leaving marks in the silvered grass under our feet.

i thought that if we started down the green we would end up in heaven.

we never quite got there but we did walk on air.

i've lived and breathed so long now it seems nothing could possibly have gone by unnoticed.

on the other hand.

routine

i wake up. i am in seattle in an apartment with my current san francisco housemates. it is 11am. there are two pairs of glasses on my bedside table: both are wire-framed but one pair is shaped like the glasses i wear now and the other looks just like my old round glasses.

my sheets are flannel with pink flowers on them. i think to myself that today i can wash my blankets because this new apartment has a washer and dryer.

i walk to the kitchen where for some reason no coffee is made even though both housemates are up. i ask c when the gay pride march begins and she answers '8:30 tonight' and i say 'isn't it odd they aren't holding it during the day as usual. are we to gather shivering in volunteer park in the middle of the night after it's over?' i think to myself that the fog will be coming in and we'll be freezing.

then i ask where the parade begins and c says 'at the bottom of revolver street' and i ask isn't that on the backside of capitol hill and she says no stupid and i say well i've been away and i don't remember.

i try to get the coffee going. there are too many lightswitches.

i realize i'm still asleep. the method for waking up in one's real bedroom in a situation like this is to close your eyes and relax and let your brain switch over to waking mode. i do this.

i wake up. it is 11am. i think to myself that today i can go shopping for new sheets to replace the flowered ones since i got my insurance money last week and could afford moderately priced sheets.

i get out of bed and notice that my mouth is filled with pea gravel. i note that i can see the toilet from my room and mark this as a sign that i am really awake. but when i get to the bathroom to spit out the pebbles i see that the toilet is on the wrong wall.

i realize i'm still asleep. i close my eyes and relax.

i wake up but do not open my eyes. i think i hear music

playing outside and then remember that i can't hear anything because my earplugs are in so i reach up to take them out.

it occurs to me that when i am trying to wake up i can't actually move my body.

i realize i'm still asleep. i relax my limbs and slowly feel them falling into the position i remember being in last time i really woke up.

i wake up but do not open my eyes.

i realize i am still asleep. i relax.

i open my eyes to see jackson lying beside me on my bed which is in the air. it is 11am. i am disappointed to know that i can't really go shopping for sheets because i have work to do and that gay pride was months ago and held during the day as usual.

i see that the hall light is on where c forgot to turn it off as she was leaving earlier and am relieved to think that there will be coffee waiting when and if i get out of bed.

i realize i am really awake. i think to myself '10 more minutes' and close my eyes and go back to sleep.

jim broadcast. opt to descend.

a trojan horse

“why did you watch it if you
did not like it.”
“I thought you liked it.”

you recall a term
for violet place settings. I
picked at a dried piece of yesterday’s
supper with my thumbnail.
that one trilled note piercing
surprised me the thrush
flapping out of my throat.

dismissed from sunday school
the latchkey carpenter

at loss as to
what to repent
his trail petered out dripping pitch
whose hollow scent would stick with you
fingered your collar
turned up in style
manual transmissions
spread southeast into
spanish moss and swampland.

how do you know the mosquito is not a vector
you're not dead yet that's how

and when your mother granted you birth
and you drew the short straw
amicably limned tincture of cedar and fir
and that sentinel sat up nights
a sight for lines or tents
your ice canoe
headed out
to skate on the underside of
"his eminence in exile"
or
"seattle lsd '96'"

tenth and juniper

it was one of those moments you knew you would write
about later just because you were going to remember
exactly how it seemed the whole city had emptied out
except for the two of you and the cars that kept insisting
on running into each other out in the street. you see
the electricity was out and we lived at the corner of an
intersection of two streets each of which thought it was
the thoroughfare and so drivers coming all directions
assumed they had the right of way and this was after two
days of "severe weather" as they call it down south for
where I live now never gets severe weather except in their
imaginations so buildings had lost walls and windows and
power lines were down all over.

we had a battery powered radio because for some reason
we kept up with things like emergency kits for the home

or maybe it was because at that time I had no stereo in my car but carried around a radio cassette player and listened to the dead kennedys on a little mono speaker and I guess that was punk or it was pathetic or something there were a whole bunch of us struggling to survive our young adulthood which is difficult enough if your sanity is not in question well every single one of ours was. by that I don't mean that we drank too much and ran naked down the street but rather that we drank when we could and took whatever drugs we could afford and various ones of us either put out our lit cigarettes in our own flesh or bled ourselves in closed door rituals that at the time no one else knew a thing about or some of us would starve ourselves and others of us fall out of windows three flights up without wings.

later I heard that a number of people did not expect me to live but this was no news to me as I did not really expect to live either. on the other hand the drama itself was mostly nil and although we did not know what else to do but self-destruct we did seem not to have the full-on jones for death that would have been necessary actually to have killed any of us.

stories get written of sordid city lives where he drinks too much and hits her and next door they shoot up between police raids and whore themselves out to pay for the habit and all the shit that goes on and has gone on and will always ever go on but no one yet has written about what it is like to come out of the suburbs slightly damaged and keep oneself on the borderline between respectability and everything your mother meant when she talked about that book she saw once that she knew was evil just by looking at it no one writes about part time jobs held one after the other and never once being fired but always at some point simply walking out because you could not stand it anymore not that anyone was cruel to you or harassed you or threatened you but you knew that simply doing the job was going to kill you if you kept going in even though it probably never had and never will kill anybody else.

we poured out of long paved or concrete driveways down into the sidewalked city where it was actually more likely that we could survive in close quarters than inside the insides of insulated isolated punctual ranch homes although friends and family would wring their hands over rumors of living rooms turned into ever-evolving performance art and imaginary snuff films the stuff of ad hoc scripts pulled from short lifetimes of mundane abuse. whether we were bored to tears I cannot remember so much as being overcome with long-term futility as though it were the only possible conclusion. thus boredom signals but less than half with the rest jostled by a heterogeneous headache of a party thrown between couch sitting resigned and drunken bottleneck punctuated meandering rage.

in the mornings I would carefully layer my body with two, three, four shirts as though dressing a future wound. clothing chosen from secondhand wire hanger racks for hue and quantity of fabric only style did not matter. this particular apartment was full of overflow from the one other corner in the city where those of us who appreciated architecture without right angles found places to our liking and this one building stood isolated on a street mainly of small businesses and slightly more upscale housing but still we often opened our front door to have fall in a homeless sleeping body which we would try gently to prop up so that we could close the door but we didn't kick them out everyone's got to sleep somewhere.

now I would worry about a burning cigarette in the hands of someone barely able to stay conscious but this was before the fire so fire was not yet possible as far as I could tell it happened to other people.

it was so dark that night without streetlights or neighbor lights or even ambient citylight bouncing back to the ground from the low rumbling clouds until the lightning sent brilliant shards crashing through windows otherwise completely opaque and we could hear the storm approaching on the radio which if you tune to the amplitude modulation band will register with a crackle of interrupted order every strike within fifty miles or so and after some time of listening to staccato of radio waves ripped apart each louder and longer than the last until finally the flickers at the horizon began to play in time with the bursts from the speakers and although I could play a burning of atlanta metaphor I will just stop short and note that a certain karma plays itself out between the clash of the warm gulf waters and the cold arctic air every summer and spring but do the tv preachers ever seem to notice this no only if a storm manages not to destroy a church will anyone be able to make out god's hand in any of it.

her mother lived in an apartment not that far away but far enough that there was electricity and carpet and television and a refrigerator and air conditioning and the sofa bed we slept on that night and even though I would rather have been underground where things like tornados cannot really come after you the simple dispersal of light from functioning lamps seemed sufficient storm cellars as though their circles of enlightenment would send an implacable whirlwind winding off in another direction when it saw us gathered there for comfort.

whether any came near I cannot say though I suspect if I do not recall waking to a roar we were never in great danger. I slept very soundly and had to get up and go to work the next day and now I cannot remember if this was the same storm that was followed by yet another line of storms if it was that same day that same year when a squall line raced across alabama the entire morning and entered georgia by noon and was upon us by 2pm I had my eye on which ditch to dive into across the parking lot from the strip mall warehouse I was working in which would probably have killed us all if the blanket-issued warnings had rung all the way true to my imagination which had an unbroken undulating line of twisters reaching from Columbus to Rome and advancing mindlessly towards fields and cities swirling tentacles of cloud and thunder reaching down to tap the earth and decide who was going to die that day.

I never quite understood the architecture of the deep south in that almost no protection from tornadic storms is built into any building on purpose. some are partially underground so you can always take cover in the basement if there is one but in many there is no basement at all and barely even a foundation especially alarming is the number of cementslabbed, corrugated steelwalled, open floored, flat roofed warehouses in which a worker has no protection whatever from flying, usually sharp metal debris and no place to shelter from the winds themselves. that was the sort of warehouse I worked in then and why I thought if I heard a roar behind us—we faced east; they usually come from the southwest—I was going to jump off the loading dock and drop myself into the ditch across from us about fifty feet.

the sky darkened and the air raid sirens sounded and we waited and although the trees did themselves blow in violent circles nothing much more happened than usual large hail explosive lightning and that still green sky that tells you something somewhere is developing into something you'd rather not see or hear or touch. when the air pressure drops your body will tell you that you are in danger and I have run before in front of mud tinged clouds bunching up and circling around and I have sat in the hallway while bolts hit the ground and trees all around the house and I have listened to a deluge made concrete by balls of ice as big as my fist but the one thing I dreaded seeing has still only come upon me in nightmares.

now that I am old I can tell them what to do when I see them but at the same time I am never surprised when they show up which renders the scene at once more and less tense rather than stare one down right into its column of occulted terror I tell myself that they disappear when I look away which is true but I still don't know what lives inside of them and cannot persuade myself to find out even when I know the dreamscape is internal to me and is no bodily threat.

it may be that the primary trauma will only ever dress up and that there would be nothing to see in there but terror itself absolutely sheer so that even if it were invisible there is no opening the eyes to it without losing one's sight or something more dear.

it would not be entirely inaccurate to suppose that the maw at the eye of the cyclone is that of saturn himself or more accurately jehovah voraciously gulping down his children into eternal torment in the fire of his own creativity the reverse narrative of life arising out of the swamps on an island of rock accreted from dust expelled by exploding stars having run their course as ovens where births matter itself from itself after gathering itself to itself the sun you know does not think through the consequences of what it is doing but ejects daily enough energy to keep us spinning for another three billion years.

where we were forged there will we be consumed again but what they got wrong what they forgot to tell me is that the horror show they cast from the mechanical procession of matter and energy is only a dream of an ego that assumes its immortality which is to say which grasps at life as though it wanted to witness its own destruction. death is a bed of flowers loam and moss and the draught of dreamless sleep whereas hell is the waking hallucination of he who refuses to let go even when it would be the most compassionate gift he could bestow upon himself and everyone around him.

to protect me from death they gifted me with a livid riot of careening razor edged shrieking demons surrounding a shapeless yet grinning face made of gristle and cavities. remember this when you tell your children what god does to little girls who lie. then act surprised when they complain of visions of a future hostile and deformed.

logic

so. p and ~p? she asked.
yes. p and ~p. said I.
then thought better:
the question: p or ~p?
which makes possible their articulation but the question
itself which forms the hinge between them without
discretely choosing and thereby making good sense.
the promiscuous question.
that is what I meant to say.
that that that that that that that
always falling down on the job.

comment

procedures exist:

protocol

steps

instructions

manuals

rules

one pint.

if you count them out they equal thirty at most.

one. two. three. four. five.

you get the idea
the idea gets you
we'll have those pressed and folded and wrapped in the
blue paper

you see?

how many now wasn't that simple can dance on the head
of a pin
feet pierced cartilage tangled in threads of steel

I thought it might help.

a tuesday lost when the sirens did not go off at noon

how'd it get to be five.

self comfort: put your feet on a stool
close to you so your knees are pulled up
put your elbow on your knee
with your arm bent towards your chin
lay your forehead in the crook of your elbow
and wait.
when it comes time,
lay your hand on the back of your head.
weep silently.
do not wipe any drops from furniture or clothing or floor:
let them soak in and evaporate on their own time.

gods and rumors of gods
stand by while the heavens slowly
slowly spin down to rest.

in my neighborhood a cat is lost. the signs up may summon cats from places where they were not lost and waited for nothing like a sign except for that of rain or a stir from underneath the loose concrete where smaller things do very little waiting but much watching.

neither they nor you nor I will end up anywhere.

atomic dustbin

there was this thick volume on world war II always sitting on the coffeetable thus I guess it was a coffeetable book which although I cannot remember a time when this book was not there I do remember the first time that I read it from cover to cover. it had pictures. it had pictures of everything and by that I mean the things you wanted to see and the things you would rather not have seen but in my insulated six-year-old immortality none of them struck me particularly one way or the other. it was however the first time that I realized the germans were the bad guys but this is not necessarily about the germans even if things in a way got started with them but all while growing up I was told how german I was and thus even so early on it was with some shock that I discovered it was not something to be inordinately proud of.

I left it that way for a reason.

this book was what made world war II the beginning of history for me. as though it were sitting there to make sure I knew the defining event of the century as soon as I was able to know about anything. I've never asked why we had it or what was the motivation behind buying it and placing it on the coffeetable where anyone at all could leaf through pages of corpses bulldozed into ditches and watch hands fused to the time of 8:15 and the sores and the burns and the footprints in the concrete of where buildings used to be and limbs torn off and the bunks upon bunks filled with bodies barely occupying space and only making faintest gestures of living and ripped up scraps of cars and people and the blasted earth shorn of both vines and dirt and of crawling things still crawling and this was all in the coffeetable book which shared its designated place with Ladies' Home Journal and Good Housekeeping and McCall's all of which taught me about sex before my mother had a chance to say anything on the subject but still I was dismayed to find out what it actually consisted of.

I should point out in case you have forgotten that I was a girl and girls tend to be dismayed when they first find out what is popularly understood as "sex." that is I can say that to the extent that I was a girl I was dismayed and to the extent that I can then speak for girls we are all dismayed or we were all dismayed or you were dismayed or at least I was. if you think about it you can probably figure out why this might be. this is before anyone was to have had at. without asking. so it was not that. not yet.

what's the use of descriptors. I will let you know when I get to the other side I will send you a sign and finally we will have our answer to what comes after and don't they all say that and don't we then never hear a word. it's the question we get wrong and subsequently the answers are but moments away from that kind of lunacy that does not satisfy the romantic in us but rather tries to kill it. why do we squish bugs out of reflex or whose reflex is it that does the squishing through us. what do you mean we white man.

in another book the book that lived downstairs in what was called a family room on the blueprints but turned into this extra room that we did not know quite what to do with as the living room upstairs held most of our living adequately including the tv until we got the color tv and put the black and white downstairs and then at some point and I do not remember the etiology for this but at some point a color tv appeared downstairs too for I remember watching movies on it while my friends came and went through the downstairs sliding glass door bearing beer and other devices for amusement to what would have been the consternation of my parents had they known unless they did know and preferred not to say which turns out to be the etiology of a lot of things quite unrelated to tv.

in this book which also included pictorial narratives depicting the reasonable yet miraculous recovery of emotionally disturbed individuals after the application of modern psychiatry and I pored over these somehow recognizing my future which turned out not always to respond to science and wasn't it in the eighteenth century that we thought we were on the verge of knowing everything and wasn't it in the 1950s that we thought we had just about finished the project begun in the salons and isn't it interesting that the encyclopedia to end encyclopedias will be infinitely modifiable and thus never be finished and how long did it take us to come to realize that but this book was a child of modernity and thus the optimism with which Bob greeted his wife after he was cured leapt out of the picture and gave me hope even before I realized I would need it. after the psychiatric triumphs the section of this book that fascinated me most but no I lie the sections that next fascinated me the most were those on the various physical illnesses that we could now treat and how and the long section on infantile paralysis one of whose symptoms was difficulty in swallowing and I with my preternaturally strong gag reflex always was a little scared that I had polio but as time went by and I did not die over and over I figured I was ok but I'd say that after those sections at least I never could quite understand the one about the flash and how to avoid radiation and how ducking under the wall holding the window you saw the flash through would save you from this thing and finally I asked what it was but I do not remember the answer except to the extent that it was probably so bad that it wasn't even worth worrying about because how can you worry about instantaneous oblivion and at that age that meant less than nothing to me which is not so different from what it means now but now I understand the consequences a bit better which is to say not at all. so because I was young I left it for the adults to worry about and this is how I grew up in the crosshairs without noticing anything unusual.

war then was like baseball in that I thought that there was always a war and that you kept track of who was winning by the casualty counts given like a scoreboard on the nightly news and the pictures of helicopters over jungles and picking up the shards left of soldiers or circling above the ash rings of places where people had lived so strange I did not even know how to comprehend how far away they were or how they could talk to one another or know which hand to use the fork in or conceive of a chair or the airplanes overhead and how strange a thing tv was or should have been which did not make an impression on me because you see the most remarkable thing about the footage from vietnam was that I assumed it was exactly what always had happened and always will happen every day in some part of the world and I suppose I was not that far from wrong but exasperatedly now I shake myself and yell that's not normal but you know I'm not so sure of that anymore either. I know a man who says Auschwitz is still happening and always has and always will and I suspect he is right but that Auschwitz is not something that you can actually see which makes it that much worse of course.

one question I'd like to ask the book that lived downstairs is whether it took seriously its own assertions that after whatever Auschwitz or Hiroshima occurred at any particular time that there would remain hands with which to sift through the ash for at some point it became clear to me that no one really thought that or that we all knew this but pretended that diving into the doorway would save us from anything worse than a 7.2 but then at the same time I was also taught that only a heartbeat lay between me and eternal torment so long as I stubbornly chose to remain among the non-elect so it was sometimes difficult to know whom to take seriously.

in my childish credulity I believed them all.

what was the difference between holocaust and hell after all. not much except hell was said to last longer. if I believed at any moment the world could make its last hairpin turn into the last judgment and plunge me headlong into the lake of fire what difference did a few Russian warheads pointed at me make. really what were they thinking of threatening us with hell if we died and with the day after if we survived. terror exerts its discipline not to mention its little hells on earth.

the cover drill consisted of huddling under your desk but we were never told what we were hiding from. I kept waiting for some vague earthquake or whatever might make the ceiling tiles fall as it was not at all clear how our desks were to function as protection. these were the metal and wood jobs with the cavernous space underneath the seat for books and until sixth grade you sat in the same desk in the same room all day every day through the whole year and the space you sat on became filled with pieces of paper and spiral notebooks and pencils and small toys snuck in until on the last day of school they passed around the round metal waste-basket to shovel your desk out into and although it seemed an endless mess somehow the whole class' worth of mess fit into the wastebasket. still it seemed likely that at least by christmas time there was enough mass in the space underneath the seat to act as counterbalance to whatever it was that was supposed to fall on your desktop to keep it from simply tipping over and bumping you on the head. by high school of course your belongings were smushed into your locker and you changed rooms every forty-five minutes and the cover drill had evolved into three blasts on the electronic bell but there was still nothing to do but get under the desks which were now wire and formica and more likely to be hurled into you in the event of a cataclysm of moderate energy than to save you from whatever it was that was attacking the two of you.

I was still not sure what we were hiding from although I had my suspicions. my brother was on safety patrol because he was an even bigger dork than I was. it was not clear to me whether they thought the drill was supposed to help us to learn to do anything useful but they did spend a lot of time pretending they were storm chasers.

the tornado drill was something entirely different.

there was that one day dark as midnight at 9am and the pounding of hail but at least we knew what that was. this did not help me at all as I was far more terrified of tornados than of the nameless predator that couldn't find you under your desk.

I tried something different at first. I tried something different but typical and being typical it turned out not to be topical which is the bind really whenever I sit down to do this and when you think of it the blast o butter popcorn on the shelf seems to know better what to say than I do and there isn't any of it that can be anything but a joke sort of like the sort we bantered back and forth that day after we awoke to the back wall on fire and ran out in the dark yelling at the firemen that the fire was in the back where you couldn't see because from our perspective they were just sitting there while the building was being consumed and suddenly we remembered that we had not grabbed the cats first like you always think you will and the photographs but when you see orange flickering outside your window as you struggle to get your pants on all you worry about further is a shirt and shoes before the window breaks or the fuel tank on that motorcycle that parks outside explodes and that's it you beat it out of there and then you stand and watch after it occurs to you.

the cats lived but smelled like smoke for some time. don't cry.

Nietzsche declared that the atom was a myth interestingly enough but at the time he thought of it as a stable modicum of known matter rather than a paradoxical bunching of energy as though a snowflake around a bit of dirt. of course the atom is neither of these things but not the one and made of several instances of the other but of course that is only what we can say about it at this point in time and later on they will laugh at us in our naïveté.

I walked down the street.

what he meant of course is that the atom in its nineteenth century indivisibility was not going to turn out to be anything like we thought at first and I guess then he was right insofar as locating the final ground of being goes. that there is energy enough in it to eradicate whatever little scrap of knowing there is is no surprise but once the knowing is eradicated surprise will be all that is left and even then only if the circumstances arise again where those little bundles can organize themselves into consciousness and that seems unlikely even on the scale of billions.

I would venture that we are the only ones here either the very first or that nominal intelligence sequentially snuffs itself out when it gets to a certain point and therefore all there is at the moment.

while walking down the street I remarked that my remarking lived the instant of its own death which came immediately after. one hundred conversations at least and only two sentences of each that I can recall and thus lend coherent being over time. the rest they went on and so did I. this life in passing.

I still do not know what evil consists of but I do know

that impermanence is at its mercy and therefore we have only to hope that evil knows something of mercy. it may be that to die for the sake of death is the only possible final gesture but that in between one death and another everything that is prone to everything else crowds in for its share.

number forty three

intractably gaping
lusting for the fist
the gavel
stone tablets for trail sign
deftly composed ache for promises outlined with daylight
not hidden in the future
but foretold to the very second where
waits to spring
unawares

who would put nothing on paper
except a tic
waiting for its next moment
no ear for revelation

have a look outwards at midnight
curtains rent years shining that

we don't even believe we can see
a heavenly host instead
we cry once out of infancy and into the thickets of language
wherein roam pronouncements and the assurance of
judgment and justice
where such notions had scarcely any propriety at all save
for the breath of their being said
the breath which gives up its hold on the world its bid to
still for an instant

god's kingdom this
and
god's kingdom that

if god is in the details it is because details like xeno's
paradox proliferate at the microcosmic scale where
infinitely speech betrays its initial wish to hold the thing
to not only approach but to seize zero
instead an incantation that trails off only as we pass
through it
the ledger that counts infinity and places us in correspondence
with death
the differential of the gasp

this most proximal angel
rather than raising hell
destroys heaven out of compassion for the devil

who arrives without form naked with begging bowl
that we might vanish unclothed is the evil we must take
on if god is love after all if in love we are to dream of
shattering tablets leaving them
ruined, amorous, exchanging glances.

refraining from content or pointing at weathermen

a car dealership closes on fourteenth street disgusted but
clamoring for starry-eyed decorous lechery crisply ushered
into red blaring sirened silence. cavernous swell you toss
coins excoriated rumors due north northeast duly noted
deep chested my heart's rhythm jumpy since we scrambled
ten of us fifty of them the once bustling square in cities
tenderfaced and broken.

drifting on the frozen street mailboxes in peril but only
kissed lightly so we turned and returned until june's hail
and lightning made the hair on my arms stand on end. franz
marc foreordained. notice words leaned heavily filigreed
scaffolding with coffee for unemployed engineers.

first trace. first center with wheat or feathered earth
crumbling orbit decayed and toothsome. fastened recreated
bulleted and justified right where light makes night and

snakes through embankments of leather unencumbered.

ribald showers underscored with shadowy pieces of
shattered knifeblades entrenched between concrete
and coldpress fibered glass. you'll not find wharves until
flashing terraces fluoresce at the meeting of sun and
moraine.

what I meant was culpability or basal metabolism. you
there: heretic clad deftly left of pneumatic traumas or
plated temples at least at last slated and labile. entranced
flint etched remnants still writing. pugilist. tarnished.
drapes counting and tipsy. shred monotony. dash smartly
east with impending fog.

one last ditch.

the myth of representationalism

tin-eared sailor pokes at dying embers left in the street or
the broken stone embryology failed to account for the
strings of epochs blown in burial notices

standing expertly amid your country of origin
dwindling trinkets burst defiled or gutted for intentions if
you would tunnel aghast and scandalous.

a lexicon falters from skinned knees
expanded under the laws of torque applied stridently
unknowing
sold not to she who carries sufficient arms
and coasting bridges but darker shelter in winter
there before sea stacks in red rock glyphed
with stark dregs
lest catacombs issue in direct song
reckon on powdered ledgers

mockingbirds kingfishers voles dragonflies
ten sundered wards
at profligate solvency

you'll depict cracked earth begrudgingly
while underfoot
clandestine velocity thunders unchecked

he pulls his punches or entertains seditious villages
declining in sync
candled leeway covets uncelebrated yield
lie mistaken daily accompanied side to side
I could have died yet brazenly mystified
resolve enters briefly
panned and teary-eyed

lost reserve an entire brigade swings wide
precise
fiery oxygen-borne
eyes closed
scattered flickers
careening holocene
stilted lean
soundtrack stricken
dusted stake
sliver thickens stirred sentience
crucibles totter restive lake

insect gods

having told the story about the moving and the always wanting to go away true to the very kernel of the story itself the story itself still seems untold although it is but the bare beginning and the background noise always like the way the radio records every lightning strike between here and there when you were getting new york or philadelphia it was not the programs themselves but the way they were broken up by the noise that distance itself imposed that was compelling and that being in love with that noise with that promise of distance yet ahead the truest comfort there where the air itself was too close and the way you had to open your window wide at night and still not garner any cooling breeze because there is no breeze unless under a thunderstorm from june until october but the heat and the moisture would crowd through the screen with the chirps and whirrs of a million crickets and beetles and grasshoppers and flying things too small to see but large enough to hear transparent wings beating the air at frequencies that would produce a tone rather than only flapping and above that the three things that can still make me cry the sound of a bobwhite a whippoorwill or a mourning dove or all three in alternation and between them and the insect civilizations springing through the night I could imagine that elsewhere was not only out on the highway where in winter you could see the headlights grow and the taillights fade but out in the woods even twenty feet from your window were worlds you could never know anything of in an intimate sense I mean more often than not I could figure out what the cat was saying but these others were foreign tongues and wings and legs in my ears but they too sang of someplace other than the place I was standing or sitting sweating over the radio trying to find a station in spanish or canadian french and I remember one evening as the dark took over the backyard I stood in the driveway and sang to the woods every sad song I knew one after the other and then repeating thinking there were ears unlike mine yet like mine waiting for word that made sense and somehow I knew that song was more understandable than say a speech or even a prayer waiting for some reply which came so subtly it is almost as if it did not either.

for clarification it was not god I was looking for in the wordless clamor of finite beings except insofar as god is dispersed into the soundwaves themselves and every moment is exhausted in the trill and the snap or insofar as god is the unconscious of the very sounds themselves or insofar as god is the enfolding of the alimentary canal of a cricket all of which are possible but for them the name of god most likely not the most likely sounding name.

opium wars

I was waiting for that one communiqué that would tell me that what I sought was waiting for me on the kitchen table or that I could get it from the man in the red hat standing beside the gate and without having to ask in spanish. it was true that although one could buy anything one wanted within a mile of my house I was too shy to do other than send money to dubious addresses hoping to get the stuff mailorder. it worked some of the time or even most of the time but the real problem was the extended period of anxiety which otherwise would have worked itself out between the man you give the money to and the man you get your packet from. then the first swallow and within an hour you had your answer.

or so I fantasized. the fact is one probably can't get just what one wants on my street but only something of a magnitude worse and it was this fact that took the shine off the fantasy and with my bashfulness kept me from looking anyone in the eye from sixteenth street to eighteenth although I hoped to glean from a sneaking glance what any one of them might have for sale. they bore no signs.

one writes in the past tense hoping for that stately patina of history and the antiseptic barrier it lends against the puddles of street muddied water that trickles out of the one alley where there are gaping holes in the pavement for the remnant of municipal cleaning efforts to drain into and where gathers during daylight hours a knot of people milling about papersacked and shrouded not going anywhere or doing anything other than just exactly what they want to do. occasionally one spies a magnificent half naked body there and at other times nothing but the crush of nakedness itself hung in thin drooping sheets between three-wheeled shopping carts and awnings once blue but now gray and full of holes. have you got a cigarette steps into your path wielding shame for covering shame hostile and resigned.

such that I have thought of buying a pack to carry with me although myself I do not smoke.

in fact I rarely leave my room. and there is not much of poetry to be written from pillules rattling in the bottom of a brief amber tube please let there be twenty more. what separates us. well it is that door and perhaps a job although what I have could hardly be called a job as the balance of accounts rushes away from me in the wrong direction ever skyward.

so I can give you no conventionally sorry story except as they unfold here between unremarkable walls unremarkable as much for their clean white paint as for their absolute replicability. make your way around the world you will pass through one wall and then another wall and another and another and another and another and another and another and between them it so happens: it so happens over here that one faints on the couch and that over there one slams their hand in the door and that over this way are a number who sleep in the throes of their own dreams and sweat and legs that chafe at the sheets tucked too tightly at the foot of the bed. I speak in the abstract but mean precisely this and that is that for three days my ankles pled to be borne up in silk and cotton hammocks that would hold them exquisitely still and immune both to gravity and the quickening electrical signals that ran unchastened down through them.

it was not enough to sink into the sheets. you remember don't you they said but it was a good tired and how the bed received you but my feet were tossed about unkindly. at ten my legs ached nightly.

I wonder at the rate of recidivism. I have a friend who

whispers in my ear to go for it as though living vicarious that one time on the edge of sleep when the well-being of the universe seemed to depend upon my hand suddenly springing away from the bed to whack the wall and then stay upright dazed yet sure that it had done the right thing. I was amazed at its impetuousness. it proclaimed itself drunk for one brief moment the archetypal stroke of fate and lightning and whatever else rises up from the earth to beckon heaven but the short of it is I had slammed my finger in a window days earlier and it was the same hand that rushed to meet the wall at twilight bruising and bemused. all the passion of fourteen ran itself out of my arm into the plaster.

for who is the last of us to fall asleep but one who lives always at the brink of fourteen when the spirit still ranged anarchically between rule and freedom. the bruising got worse. what could one expect but exactly that and exactly where the articulate cement meets obdurate the bruised hand.

some nights later I awoke with arm stretched out to the ceiling reaching for something forgotten in the half-dream which preceded my awakening. in some circles they say you must hit bottom before you can get better but things are working out all nonlinearly for me in that the bottom was the bottom of something else long ago and ever since then it has been up up up although occasionally sideways or in a circle in the air that your hand draws following sleep's solemn logic where significance alone bares itself as the obscene joke upon which your life depends.

as I was saying the story will not be sorry as the joke for the moment which brought me to my salvation was not a moment of pathos and awakening except to the cruel force of salvation and so I sidestepped it and found that having accomplished this once you only have to keep doing it as long as you also wish to say anything for saying anything implies coming down on one side or the other whereas to move laterally between choices does away with the whole necessity of making a choice but most don't see it that way. it is said he will spit out the lukewarm to which I reply how delightful to escape being devoured.

I carry a business card. I am not in business and nothing I do is categorizable in a rolodex but in case I feel the need to give someone evidence that I consider myself an entity I carry these cards and give them out at those moments when it seems like I should. so far as I can tell no one has ever thought it necessary to refer to one later on or that is I have yet to receive a phone call that began you gave me your card. I on the other hand have referred to a card like this more than once but generally it is only to check that the memory I have of being handed a card is truly a memory and not the recollection of something I made up. rarely do I do anything more with the information on the card than establish that it exists.

but so I have thought about carrying a business or calling card with me that I can leave with strangers at the end of the conversation or journey or meal or interminable line and this card would say you have just met a gay transsexual drug addict. wasn't he nice?

for an ambassador for all that is set to destroy society need only engage one of the embattled ones in conversation to make it clear that society is in no danger of being destroyed and is in fact the one thing that we could not possibly lose as long as conversations are being held in one quarter or another which they are even in hell. sure some of the rules could stand to be loosened and a modicum of chaos would be good for the terminally uptight but the craven among us will still say please and thank you when they want the salt. you don't need a nuclear family to keep the graces operating as they should.

down at the shop the atmosphere is so nonchalant that the old man sits under the streetlight at the intersection, a busy intersection, but one where one minds one's own business unless you are paid not to but that sort seems to show up so rarely that no one gives them a thought certainly not the old man with his altoids tin full of little chunks of the black as they distinguish it down there from the white, the only two things they sell except chiba which refers to something illegal but I have not discovered what.

gathered around him are hungry looking people. my middle man tells me not to stand too close so as not to draw attention but this old guy is sitting on a stool behind the traffic signal box it is true but in full illumination nonetheless carefully cutting and wrapping—and neatly burning the wrappers shut tight with a match—and everyone and no one knows he's there sitting calmly like the jewelry makers and the sellers of other people's lost items down by the big shopping mall where half the nation experiences san francisco.

only certain people can approach him. a priest doling out wafers to those who kneel at a respectful distance from the altar. I find my guy and he takes me over, about halfway, says stand here and then goes on up to place my order. 'he's got to cut it from the gram.' 'oh just give me the gram. how much is it?' but the communication breaks down and I pay for a gram that weighs 0.5g when I get home to my scale. curses. well I'm out ten dollars cause I woulda paid forty for half a gram cause I had only twenties no change. next time I'll be more clear.

except there's not supposed to be a next time or at least not anytime soon. I have to keep an eye on the scene in the meantime but from across the street as they know me now and I can't get through that particular crowd without being pestered to buy something which I usually do out of courtesy. you gonna walk through the middle of all that with money and knowledge you oughta buy.

there's always someone there. this was the first time I'd seen a little booth set up on the street. usually it's already cut and in pockets although you never know whose pocket it's going to be in. this one guy seems to direct the whole operation like a sidewalk receptionist routing phone calls to the appropriate party. he has a distinctive look—a little underbite, a little gray hair, always the same pea coat and looking you in the eye saying what you want so everybody comes to him and gets sent or led to the pertinent person depending upon what they are there for. sometimes he has it himself and I don't know if the main guys give it to him and leave or if he has his own supply. the quality varies wildly and you always hope it's going to come in a balloon because when it does it's usually pretty good.

the market itself extends across the street over into another brightly lit plaza where no one should be doing the sort of business everybody does there. no one is subtle about what they are looking for and sometimes I'll get two dealers or a middle man and a dealer or two middle men and they start shouting about which of them saw me first. I play the diplomatic high class junkie who can give each of them a bill to keep them from killing each other but the shouting continues as I walk away from the bright lights to the back route home.

types at flies

listing on the port side sliding
past bergs two thirds unknown I have heard
wait here at length you will be along
the rail head bent to trace a line
to the vanishing point five feet distant
silhouettes against a heaven red with hints
of release in silver baring
its menace at arms innocent and prone
to attacks of doubt
drove an entire school from circling
the black figure under a full moon
drew our eyes skyward
shooting rockets flared
into particles of flame returning to earth
is never as straightforward as might be thought.

a practiced nightmare.
couriers at full gallop.
crouched tipping a tin cup into the remnant of rainwater
secured us against thirst.
drosophila living in a glass jar.
gracefully angling across a minute expanse.
no longer veiled rage
pulled round your shoulders a musty larval-scalloped blanket.
boldly maneuver stakes shivering
rheumatic joints arrived naked and scarred.
stereotyped behavior driven in a standard
set of feral gestures
at a rock cairn indicating our destination.

notation.
cylindrical.
iron filings.
ionic or
lenticular.
a sea change sundered.

directories do not begin to comprehend
the destiny of your soul considered
five seals or seven.
falsified evidence.
diverse litanies written in brittle cadence.
trouble sulked crestfallen

soldiered benignly
underground
cistern
leaching
chlorine.

tachyon

feeling randomly out of sorts I remembered that one cause of that nonchalant fatigue that will not sleep but will not wake up either is hormone lag so I got out my syringe and my vial and as there was enough left in the vial for one and a half doses decided to take the whole bolus and see if I'm bouncing off the walls in three days. it would be a nice change. must remember to put off next shot a bit lest I overdose myself and some of the testosterone be turned into estrogen.

it does that, you know, if you take too much over a period of time. every generation of transsexual men discovers this fact for themselves and passes it on as received wisdom that happens actually to be true.

but so hormones or not and whatever else there is neuro-chemically to blame your mood on you still have to live it and since every state of mind has a physiological substrate it's only a matter of some of them being more available to manipulation than others that makes one any less 'real' than another which is to say none of them are less real than any other but some are engineerable if you do the right thing at the right time. part of the problem is never knowing exactly the right time because the physiology is a complicated little motherfucker of a problem like the other day I thought I needed a lift so I drank one of those soda pop energy drinks with ginseng and was dropped like a rock into a three-hour nap sitting slumped in my chair narcoleptic. as uncanny as coffee on a day when you've not had enough sleep: these particular stimulants only tell you if you are awake enough to utilize them and if not they put you under for adjustment. I wonder if I did speed now if the same things would happen.

speed is not the problem now though. the trick will be not getting off the train at 16th street and not walking around the block once or twice with my eyes shifting from face to face. that's the look I think. they all ask me what I'm looking for these days anyway even if I'm not looking but just walking to the station. you don't have to know them and they don't have to know you but they know.

where there is smoke

when it came my turn to be thrust momentarily past death's boundary into the excesses of fate rather than simply being threatened therewith as recompense for having the temerity to exist this last had already put to silence my protestations of innocence even though nothing else had any claim on me. the rudeness of this violation set a small crowd of us to flight. were they to return we would be forced to find again faith in well-being which faith is misplaced on this earth by entities with self-composed but broken surfaces.

one might begin to ask if the bond between life and death is the affinity of matter and energy for each other and whether the oscillation between them is not that which batters raw tissue against the concrete for to be bound is to be as cold as cement and as warm as a black cat in the sun while aware that the furnace will always crack untempered glass.

the dead man in me is all too conscious of the inroads made by microscopic phages which live upon his skin waiting for him to discard it. It is not so much that I can feel the mites in my eyelashes when they bite into still living flesh as it is that intimate blood vessels deliver the shrill notes of oxygen and nitrogen from my lungs to membranes dreaming in saline up until they are scraped clean by the bite of my own breath returning me piecemeal to ash while warming the inside of my sleeping bag where I curl into myself for company and comfort.

not at the stake but in slumber every stroke that dries thirsty clay to the point of immolation so that feet may step and hands touch emits a wisp of curled light its torn edges whirling off into intricate complications of shallow trails dug across abraded dry washes of lightly seared shoulders and knees.

stopping breathing in would stop it but there is no stopping breathing in or none that I am yet prepared to give up even for the emollient that would be humus and water.

a day in the life

my first ever diagnosis was schizoid personality disorder. I am pretty sure that it was derived from my habit of sitting on the couch and staring intently at the carpet while I fished around in my head to the answers to my psychologist's questions. a simple one like how are you doing could leave me sitting for five minutes trying to descry just how it was I was doing because in the moment I could not find anything like a clear delineable concept to wrap around the event horizon that was my internal being. and determining how it *was* once located was at least two orders of magnitude beyond my powers of observation.

when you are in your family when you are small you think everything that occurs there is normal. naturally families are all a little different but the platonic form of family issues from the conditions surrounding you when you are so young that your world is constituted by the house, the yard, the driveway, the car, and the places the car takes you to most often like ballet lessons or shoney's big boy restaurant or those dirt track stock car races that live at the fringes of my memory but at the time I thought it was real professional sport.

it was georgia.

if the list of my world doesn't include the people in it, what does that mean? it might mean the diagnosis was accurate I suppose. but how does one write about these things without lapsing into the narrative of childhood trauma leading to the fucked up adult you are now and how does one avoid blaming everything on mom? my current therapist knows two jokes: in therapy it's always one thing or your mother. and therapy is where you say one thing and mean your mother.

poor mom.

seriously. poor mom. she hasn't the strength of grasp on reality sufficient to be able to comprehend anything about me except that I am extremely introverted. the one thing she was able to do for me when I was little was to find me places to hide when we were at large gatherings with other families and I was growing visibly distressed at the sheer numbers of children wanting my attention. I became intimately acquainted with other people's guest rooms and offices and in the offices I especially would open the drawers one by one with great interest at the implements of orderly living and in fact I can see in these scenes the beginnings of the office supply fetish that can lead me now into office depot with as much enthusiasm as into an electronics store. I even worked for an office supply warehouse for a number of years as a young adult and although I will not go into the exact quantities of pens and paper and little organizers that I took as fringe benefits suffice it to say that I so thoroughly flunked the polygraph test they once made us take that nothing I said not even my name appeared to be the truth so they had to assume I was just crazy stressed out rather than a thief stressed out.

when I say I went silent at 15 which is not the literal truth but I'll explain in a minute but when I went silent it wasn't like anyone came after me. they let me be. few questions ask for fewer answers and so I slowly unlearned how to put together sensical answers for the simplest of introspective inquiries.

a lesser light

rigged gingerly a torn leaf
peal or pleasantly yelp ink
of your quarter-toned rustic curses
detonate ingrained turquoise purses
mischief curls trenchantly and kind
a palliative leap over land and sea
vent your torpor veiled in valerian tea

the chase was rotted leaden distilled

natal proton devil eyed
ravens appeal to riparian seeds
frankly scattered chants restore one scented road
acquainted to rainy tonnage and squalls
aching in tranquility rendered tripping
salty and silent
never vary or linger

curtains may trap you febrile
and vapor stunted defend us with maps straining or
straightforward stupor leapt outstretched
vibrantly strung why repast spells rain
rapidly made brittle versus noumenal palace

avid laurels limp venerable
damnable traces in terraced slats
liquid raster violent cherubs laugh
notoriously gaunt rings interred
stack deleterious tattered wharf rats
nepal pending voracious
seduced livid talons
tangled archive

sip dusty crystalline needle rimmed

portable villainous art for rapt jailers
eviscerate appalled droves vital limbs-slaked felon
will fashion lucky furred hymns
tournament returns burning craft
no kin in stasis
sainted ermine treads alone
guarded pale granite worn

dime store (letter to patti smith)

it does not matter to me whether or not anyone else thinks it was a good idea or whether or not it was legal at the time or whether or not it might have killed me because what it did do was put life in the shining blade of light that only squeezes itself out from my synapses when coerced by some stronger force than I myself can synthesize. I don't remember where it came from this one time or why it was that no one could join me but I having nowhere to go with it took it up to a cul de sac at the end of a new subdivision road the kind that went back into the trees before any had been felled for wood siding and before there was any room for houses or streetlights or curious windows. rather only asphalt labyrinths leading nowhere except deep into possum country so I in my yellow beetle drove around this one newly plotted and paved subdivision until no one was paying attention into a dead end pulled around with my back to the woods and turned off the headlights.

I waited. just for a little while to see if any wayward police officers were following or wondering what I might be up to but in the thick summer night heat young kids in cars did all kinds of odd things like we used to drive around a corner in one particular road and park and then pick our way down the pine banks to a river that ran without any hurry through a collection of large flat wet stones and we would hop from one to the next trying not to spill our beer and after we had gotten a little ways downstream we would exit the river and sit at the edge of water and trees and out of pockets came the auxiliary beers or the bottle of screw-top wine and there we'd be for however long we felt like it and no one ever asked us what we were doing there sitting in the dark by the water so that we could listen to what it was trying to tell us about what it was one left home for.

after several minutes had passed in the dark with maybe a moon of some proportion or another for ambient light and no one seemed to notice I was there for whatever reason on came the interior light and I would carefully pour out a small dip of powder onto my drivers license as I had not thought nor had the chance to procure a small piece of mirror or other glass surface but I did always carry a razor blade in those days as it was useful for any number of swipes at release whether in private or in common with one of the two people responsible for keeping me alive back then.

I waited. it was never clear how long it would take until it took.

whatever time it took I was always taken by surprise and then in a heartbeat that bravely kept on beating time vanished and off I would go.

time was always on my side but playing against me. racing for the finish in the leisurely space of suspended seconds.

and fifths and sevenths.

I am taken how we make our way across time meeting without meeting in spaces none could mark for we pass in the company of people who never will know us and without certain of whom we would not have been able to continue on treading place in this or that where or when. unmeasurably far but close enough that eyes can meet without meeting across an acoustically puzzling auditorium the greeting comes: "hello." my watch turns raucously around and around until it is not clear to me whether the chair itself has sat there for years waiting for me or if I have sat for years in that one chair. the word wasn't "hello" then but on "hello" I hear what they say it is to hold something in common to communicate even without the customary hello to stretch across a space that cannot be closed without killing the spark that flies from one side of it to the other. I compose another letter that I will not write and will not send but in it I put down as to how did it how was it to have survived long enough to hear this word now as it was uttered differently but a greeting all the same or not all the same or not at all like anything that had greeted me before this voice from a time I cannot yet narrate it in my memory still that raw collision of elements over my head. they will eventually out but today my mother tongue cannot apprehend them.

sitting yet still some elastic distance from the same stage where I had projected my own image until it was possible that I got to stand on one stage or another in one sort of position or another but right now I cannot decide which platform was supposed to be the one I would not leave behind all that is clear is that it seems now I must make clearer than I possibly can exactly what was going on at every moment and I do not even know what in practical or impractical terms it will do for any one of us if I succeed. only that it is necessary to gather up whatever power I might be able to scare up to speak right to the limit of what cannot be said because whatever passes for a spirit or a fate or a chance encounter with the shadow of the valley while out looking for something to keep one busy only asks that I do so and without threat but also without any apparent alternatives other than the one I have not taken again and again and again and again.

how to find words for how words found me in notes of mercurial affect run rampant out of buzzing cabinets.

what I could not figure out what to say was that I could not find quite the right words to explain to me or to you how to express a fairly complicated sense of gratitude for standing over there microphone having registered what you said and sent it pressing to my ear one more time and one more time and one more time and one more time and from some point this time or another that time at a proximity just close enough for me to have heard you summon from sleep in my vouchsafed soul the scorned transfigured child of Cain and to feel him respond to a miracle of telephonics intimating exactly as though somewhere some one of us still moved in response to the profane miracle of life on earth still listened to the voices of the gods of this world. through the membrane tympanic the faintest hope began to flare so shy but

long enough for me to lay known the knife I had at that time constantly pointed up under my own jaw.

how I had managed to keep the spirit and the flesh from

parting forever long enough to hear you say it again thirty years past time curiously unsuspended itself but no how or rather to the question one may say at the least that of the saving phrases the ones I carried close enough to the pounding in my temples that I managed not to pierce an arterial vessel ever but only scratched the surface this and a handful of others on a short stack of etched cellophane verses from no place other but that intervening distance between us kept my hand steady while I wrote the notes that were not meant for the survivors of suicide but for living eyes themselves to read and read back and forth across the orchestra pits that marked the constant variable between us once you had returned from the ghostly realm of those I was certain I had met too late ever to meet.

what I meant to say was my life will not know but it is bound up already and from now on to whatever replaces now with your surrender to your own voice and the pitched fever you sang to me over a tin-can stereo lighting a patch of pine woods. all I know to do in return is to pantomime to the beat should the beam ever hit me.

sag mir was das war

sedimented against garroted mounts
iterate rhined warbirds although surely
defects are signal wishes
archaic riots

mythologized in race worn altitudes
reciprocate and let serial hatred
air their tangled embankments
sans terror
drift under early it's noon
even now but later if convicts knead
addled urine flecked mud
itself caked hidden green ester woven
of rife ferns
enter now

internal crises have made idols crane hard

guests eat
despite untoward caterwauls kept tacitly
sewn

again greet me if rainy weather attends
so daring a soldier waits
at rest

one strike?
gratuitous arc.

postscript

the miraculous thing about language is that it always says something even when there is nothing to say. which also makes it sometimes despotic and sometimes seemingly quite helpless to do anything about anything at all for what is there to do but to talk about what happened.

I could say that I've spent my life in search of a diagnosis. today I would say that it would not matter what classification I was slipped into in the language that medicalizes what it does not know: the intricate switches that run the length of the spine and the femur and the tibia and out to tarsals and meta-tarsals so-named just as though they stood for something else but the heck of it is that no matter what one says about the charge that is borne along continuously arcing low-voltage sparks across intervals smaller than anything one can see and how all braided together like the metal grounding strap that used to sometimes hang off of the engine block like it was supposed to go somewhere but stopped short of its destination and you never knew if someone had yanked it away or if it had slowly corroded to powder at that point where the washer around the bolt was supposed to hold it close to the automobile body quietly thumping over the tar-pitched expansion seams in the concrete freeways running under a sun that prevailed over their black sticky elasticity until the tar ran in rivulets off into the grass holding nothing together anymore except your shoes to the ground.

there were no words for that and he knew it and it was not even a matter anymore of trying to work something out for himself in his head it was or was it that to enter polite society and not to ask for more than one's due one had simply that is you had to talk to them. there was no other way. in all of the universe where both potential and the real took on the blazing insignia of infinity and wore it rushing against what was frequently referred to as heaven but which chafed too at its own bindings revolting even against the patterns it etched in archaic habits ever scratching the same number again and again until what was written there was no longer the same but something like a crowd unleashed with every intention of doing nothing other than turning itself inside out with the energy that crackled from ligament to bone.

but it was not like that. if there is anything I do not know, it is that I do not know what eventual significance might ensue upon taking flint to the skull and spreading its contents on the bare rock in the sun to be read as bird's entrails might be read or offering the interior of passion itself out pounding the sidewalk or blindly sweeping the floor for spare change and pulling up dust mites and paper clips.

there was not really anything anyone could do or that is there was not really anything that anyone would do realistically one hears the lament all the time if only I had done something if only there had been something we could have done and there probably was but it would have been against all good moral and economic principle to do it. as I said you could interminably question what precisely you deserved out of it all but it is not as though you do not ask to be shown every possibility before being served up two: if whatever it is cannot retire itself to the contours of the single alternative you were taught between good and evil then whatever it is is probably demonic beyond the pale even of evil and should not be encouraged lest a message be sent to the youth of this nation to do other than nod sleepily or rather gregariously mingle on the cutting floor of what I always thought of as the film that would be made if the script were written on the floorboards of the elementary school where I walked with my satchel and waited solemnly for someone besides the deities I was offered to bear me up on their wings and away.

I cannot tell a regular story. I cannot work a regular job. I cannot hold a regular conversation. I cannot keep a regular schedule. I do not follow the regulations requiring me to hold onto my financial information for however many years it is one is supposed to do that because it strikes me as patently absurd to do so.

I cannot tell you what I was going to tell you but it is not like there is something else that I cannot tell you but more that the eyes and skin of the universe sit waiting in each of us but not even waiting to squeeze through this bottleneck where superstition and belief are both indistinguishable and incomprehensible but more than likely to kill us off because apparently what the universe cannot do is believe in itself or it is not yet intelligent enough to do so filled as it is with mute velocities whirling about and colliding and occasionally sparking that wildfire that spreads so far in such a short time that whole empires rise and fall without each other's knowledge in this far corner or that and if out of all of this there is only good and evil if workhammers are pulled as often as guns and brandished at this or that one life without a nose for wealth in the colloquial sense but that everything we need presents itself literally makes of itself a gift and no other hand driving it or giving it only warm blood giving itself up for cold blood or viscosity for capillary expansion or any of so many more possible exchanges that naming them would run off of every page and continue doing so forever the myth that one must tug at the earth and crack it and otherwise batter it being the founding tale of one of our stonebroken clan among many brought up on the hard dried mud flats of petrified riverbeds in all bad luck but now in the middle of tall trees that drip their own rain on moss and teeming loam day and night since before anyone even had the sense to write it down then why not describe a dream less impoverished before turning over to sleep sated with the radical generosity of the dirt that is not ours but only itself only.

I may have said this but I used to count the rows of planks in the tall vaulted ceiling of the sanctuary surreptitiously looking up as though that were not the most appropriate place to look given the sermon but counting them made it clear the arbitrary nature of everything that unfolded underneath it and I knew it and I knew it but it was not something enough to hold onto me when they grabbed me by the hair and dragged me to the baptismal pool I had long hair then and come to remember it was not just the walk which kept me so long from walking but it was also the dunking I had been afraid of being submerged since breathing in that lung's worth of chlorinated pool water and I opened my eyes underwater for the first time and recognized nothing but kicked harder to find the ladder we all were swimming towards and as soon as my hand found the rail and my head broke the surface I gulped in a mouthful of oxygenated relief and then began to cough and kept coughing and could not stop coughing and through nausea and chest cramp coughed and coughed and coughed and the teacher who had not noticed before taking us to the deep end that unlike the other kids I had not learned to turn my head up out of the water to breathe asked with a laugh did you swallow the whole pool.

so there was that too. underwater for even a second was too long. I started practicing in the bathtub when it became clear there was no escape.

I cannot tell you how many planks there were in the ceiling but I can tell you that I knew already that there would come a time like no time when my having sat there would be of no consequence even to the heavenly beings invoked on my behalf on a daily basis. what I did not know is that the church had no door out or rather that one church contained another church contained another and another and if there were anything at all to do it would have to be to dismantle every one of them piece by piece examining each component and setting it in random piles to be used not ever again for edifices but as recombinant DNA that might fly and take off without notice for parts unknown and find the rhythm of the time spent heading there itself granting that exuberant peace speeding not home but home speeding itself but although I have managed almost to disassemble one single church it appears to me that the next and the next and the next are each slightly bigger holding more territory more armaments and more crowds willing to die rather than see them taken down even when they know the buildings themselves obscure both sight and sound of the unbearable reach of interstellar space waiting with more patience than we may live to see for us to live to see it.

what the family bible was for

lineage
librarians
teachers housekeepers
a farmer and a farmer's wife

uncle pete he fell over a fence and died
if by fence you mean
shotgun
if by fall you mean
thumb on the trigger leaning into the blast

list
still
listless

oh I thought about it
rough outline
blood like water

good housekeeping's public service warning

baby gulps turpentine
the can dented grimy
cut out I cut it out I
meant what it said but
cannot negate signs of flame
cannot begin to exercise blame
cannot beseech your chastened shame

only

stand notice here
urge liminal sphere:
the body elastic pulled tight
plastic at agents of venture and preventure
exventure inventure abventure adventure
periventure
unventure
you spell out a lexicon
extinct
yet vindicated
diverticulated
skeletal will

while surface anomalies nameless
discomfort declination
banner waves
blinks out

rotifer
planarian
liverwort
teleost

a blank space
one cannot write
a blank space

tissue without principle
laugh hyena
gauloisie
signs hushed
potentiated
brushes uninked
no kin
shambled but
spasming in
dry heat

hydra
barnacle
droll tabernacle

abandoned demand

scouring codices postfilial relations risking impromptu nap
makeshift effigies for
divine couples who'd deny
breath plaited nearby
twist ramified
shadowy pantheon faintly inscribed
arrayed across beaten dirt floors
fascia of faces erased translating stone to air and returned

detour

to turn away
conceding
writing
desisting
writing
disintegrating ungrateful forgetful writing
twined in fields
fallow gesticule
cultivates seedless windfall

doubled over scarecrow suckerpunched cattle call

I would not have dreamed of this twenty-five years ago
when all I could tell was nothing of real consequence or
just something slightly misleading and damn it I said you'll
not fool me

do we get tired
yes we get tired
does it insinuate itself within us
yes it insinuates itself within us
is our resistance low
yes our resistance is low
or
in extracting the foot one entangles the hands and in
extracting the hands one entangles the mouth and in
extracting the mouth one entangles the knees and in
extracting the knees one entangles the ears
or
how do you keep a madman busy (answer on back)
how do you keep a madman busy (answer on back)

or
if the unconscious is structured like a language
then
what is the unconscious of language structured like?

here our ruin
pillars broken and crumbled back to the spherical
horizontal of earthbound homeostasis
I would admit the obscene
had I means to draw the screen
a borrowed throw
drapes folded wood I convulse
spare a dime sir please
edicts surgical intervention
lest we devise a word
yet too slim
for
credit
or
decree
but stretched from standard deviations
detached stranded fluvial agency
derived hence
so where

no where
any what
a hat of flame illumines
mortar and pestle and board and tassel
select elect trisected erection of desiccated sacs soft as talc
collected tins a stint tied to the mast
he stems from tainted pools

misted supplicants murmur at ear level
vole tunnels earthbound
stunned and in tears
striated
destitute
a terrier for protection
architect of resistant spells

saint therese
quicken your hounds
beckon ankle bitten cabin fever
never blacken my lanky veins several decades severed
sirens in nickel over silver
lichen over sulpher

point zero zero one per cent tracing caveward
directly curtail vast linkages greet time eyes lowered
volume one
no index
volume two
without mention
reservoir verses served in closed circles
in.
out.
between.
nets three all else muffled
we'd sell a duffel's worth of stems for thirty-nine cents
seemingly felled where an ear cast off hears little

so easy were it no lines could throw even their own ghosts
here silence has a say without breathing a word

my manhood
oh
my monkhood
oh
oh uncouth wobble of axis unsure no surname resumes
cursing below
enough lobs of pitchfire
poor slouches sobbing
before beatings certain to bruise
—or beating with batting lightly it billows
—or sobbing impoverished shed of verity instead
for straining tongue not strangulate but painting in tones
gutter bright
night interleaved with light of star neither god nor familiar
burnt figures to the right
but thin trails aged from years solar wind
elementally allied
lamented dalliance searing you there your death bed
blown to bits

still throb
stillbirthed party mask scabbard skims
milked powdered milk
limiting swallows not to consume but spew presence
crepuscular glances off clockwise current
I am not here
nor he
nor they
nor you
however we may have sailed north
details slapping the hull in icy sheets

would a fur cradle but for doubts arising history snarling
unrecognized the glass glazed over
grass staggered uphill
introducing itself a stranger
mouth full with words unbidden and dithering

thrust into the aisle he walks without feet teeth bared
against advice
devised visitation without rights
reading from a holy book cobbled together
titters
tethers
leather flayed
yelps heard through stopped ears

they stood for me
deposited terror in ladies' shoes I stuttered forward in drag
drew behind dim outline
of herds lightly pattering
a smattering of cedar
receding

folded in winter chests
stochastic reason waits
still you strike me with chords
sequestered cities sing
as though!
not yet!
unnamed!
dearest madre of empty space!

curiosity intoned dust rising at the horizon
you have a visitor
extends one smooth cold palm
a lamp toothsome pale
my paw crimson listens behind the door
rations rationalized
razors sequestered
little blue tubs
but
a lizard
feeling your shadow
will skitter

(leaning in: now?)

I'll risk another then
skilled in rustic
esoteric
mesophallic
only more so meaning
less

where asphalt takes flight one grain at a time
one tall apprentice
promise-thin
debate versified
drumming a sprite
to demonstrate scale in relation
to the sovereign
tarpaulin distills overnight dripping ringing into a parched cup
ping

ping
ping
ping

hummingbirds
hover where next you glance the angle slight but extenuating
found waiting
rusted crusaders in tin hats
attired in tongues I've seen them pass out at the altar
impaled convicts driven to the dirt chained and shoveled
dancing ataxic
sleeves woolen straining at stained wrists
hearts of powdered granite tumbled smooth
salt licks
ruminants
sterling red
crucible
blessed wheat stone broken to the hearth
intone the household spirits
we are plastered
the last to disperse pressed lightly into the earth

our feet a prayer or whispered
love
on repeat falters
I cannot tell

onscreen redress dare we tear for breath
or rest naked taken
courts martial
grout cell

serpentine
traipse
strapping pastoral
invited torpor
temporal diversion sundered
reportedly reckoning under dovetail joint

facing me arrayed in pews
damp eyed burdensome straits
of a sudden
did you not surrender
inter implicitly
rein caressing the carotid corridor
clotted hide soaked voiceless troubadour
collects bones in orbit
rumble off this way
hashed outfitted flickering serrated steel
lateral precision
marks
emits time

or

mister
thanks

trim limping captive skin
simple fatigue or complicated delicate gaffe
or vestige on the highway going east we faced west
specifically the ocean turns inwards
begins to chew its own entrails

the seawall
a long sigh
draw your bead along the ragged concrete
deranged tent city wardens
gathering
a single draw
saving receipts

if I have to interject
what have I
what has I
what did I
energy charged I beam
enemies graced eyes gleam
I has but meager claim
searches no secret chamber for no idols
I does not meet itself between syllables
nor hidden behind already secret inscriptions

nor will I emerge attenuated and pure after the casting off of
ruptured telecasts drifting toward some galvanized ceiling
a draft taken under
selections unaccountable
smog settles at evening

limb worth less than a broken reed
shattered chert
stars retch terrain
ratcheted debris earthbound
teach inclined ears rectitude stretched thin
a heart figures figures to reach reaches

frequently
in lower case
a fox will escape
or a lazy dog
my coat
red
threadbare

Atelos was founded in 1995 as a project of Hip's Road and is devoted to publishing, under the sign of poetry, writing that challenges conventional, limiting definitions of poetry.

All the works published as part of the Atelos project are commissioned specifically for it, and each is involved in some way with crossing traditional genre boundaries, including, for example, those that would separate theory from practice, poetry from prose, essay from drama, the visual image from the verbal, the literary from the nonliterary, and so forth.

The Atelos project when complete will consist of 50 volumes.

The project directors and editors are Lyn Hejinian and Travis Ortiz. The director for text production and design is Travis Ortiz; the director for cover production and design is Ree Katrak.

Atelos (current volumes):

1. *The Literal World*, by Jean Day
2. *Bad History*, by Barrett Watten
3. *True*, by Rae Armantrout
4. *Pamela: A Novel*, by Pamela Lu
5. *Cable Factory 20*, by Lytle Shaw
6. *R-hu*, by Leslie Scalapino
7. *Verisimilitude*, by Hung Q. Tu
8. *Alien Tatters*, by Clark Coolidge
9. *Forthcoming*, by Jalal Toufic
10. *Gardener of Stars*, by Carla Harryman
11. *lighthouse*, by M. Mara-Ann
12. *Some Vague Wife*, by Kathy Lou Schultz
13. *The Crave*, by Kit Robinson

14. *Fashionable Noise*, by Brian Kim Stefans
15. *Platform*, by Rodrigo Toscano
16. *Tis of Thee*, by Fanny Howe
17. *Poetical Dictionary,* by Lohren Green
18. *Blipsoak01*, by Tan Lin
19. *The Up and Up*, by Ted Greenwald
20. *Noh Business*, by Murray Edmond
21. *Open Clothes*, by Steve Benson
22. *Occupational Treatment*, by Taylor Brady
23. *City Eclogue*, by Ed Roberson
24. *Ultravioleta*, by Laura Moriarty
25. *Negativity*, by Jocelyn Saidenberg
26. *The Transformation*, by Juliana Spahr
27. *To the Cognoscenti*, by Tom Mandel
28. *Parse*, by Craig Dworkin
29. *The PoPedology of an Ambient Language*, by Edwin Torres
30. *The Route*, by Patrick Durgin and Jen Hofer
31. *To* After That *(Toaf)*, by Renee Gladman
32. *One Last Ditch*, by Erik J.M. Schneider

Distributed by:

Small Press Distribution
1341 Seventh Street
Berkeley, California
94710-1403

Atelos
P O Box 5814
Berkeley, California
94705-0814

to order from SPD call 510-524-1668 or toll-free 800-869-7553
fax orders to: 510-524-0852
order via e-mail at: orders@spdbooks.org
order online from: www.spdbooks.org

One Last Ditch
was printed in an edition of 700 copies
at Thomson-Shore, Inc.
Text design by Erik J.M. Schneider and Lyn Hejinian
using Perpetua for the text, GillSans for the titles, and
Georgia for the page numbers.
Cover design by Erik J.M. Schneider
and Ree Katrak/Great Bay Graphics.